FULL BELLIES HUNGRY SOULS

Making Personal Contact with God

BENNETT CHOTARD

Copyright © 2016 by Bennett Chotard

Full Bellies Hungry Souls
Making Personal Contact with God
by Bennett Chotard

Printed in the United States of America.

Edited by Xulon Press

ISBN 9781498464963

All rights reserved solely by the author. The author guarantees all contents are original and do not infringe upon the legal rights of any other person or work. No part of this book may be reproduced in any form without the permission of the author. The views expressed in this book are not necessarily those of the publisher.

Scripture quotations taken from the New Living Translation (NLT). Copyright © 1996, 2004, 2007 by Tyndale House Foundation. Used by permission. All rights reserved.

www.xulonpress.com

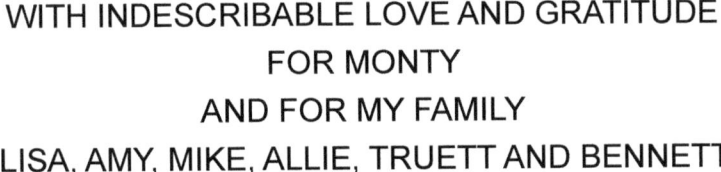

WITH INDESCRIBABLE LOVE AND GRATITUDE
FOR MONTY
AND FOR MY FAMILY
LISA, AMY, MIKE, ALLIE, TRUETT AND BENNETT

Table of Contents

Chapter 1:   Let's Talk. 9
Chapter 2:   "Bennett, are you a Kook?". 12
Chapter 3:   Refusing a Royal Invitation. 15
Chapter 4:   So Where Do We Start?. 19
Chapter 5:   Half Way There Is Not There 25
Chapter 6:   Getting Serious for the First Time. 28
Chapter 7:   Cotton Candy 32
Chapter 8:   The Secret 35
Chapter 9:   Now What?. 45
Chapter 10: Wake Up! 49
Chapter 11: Continuing Walking in the Way 51
Chapter 12: Find a Mentor 53
Chapter 13: The Bible. 57
Chapter 14: Quiet Time 62
Chapter 15: Writing Your Story. 65
Chapter 16: "Oh No!" 68
Chapter 17: Restitution. 73
Chapter 18: Prayer. 77
Chapter 19: Gratitude. 83
Chapter 20: More and More .88
Chapter 21: Every Day is Christmas 91
Chapter 22: You Are A New Creation! 95

Chapter One

Let's Talk

I was taught that becoming a Christian would make me a new creation.[1] For much of my life that certainly was not the case, for if I were a new creation, wouldn't I know it? I was just me—same ole, same ole. I needed something "new" alright; I just didn't know what. If you cannot identify with me, you probably should just put this book back on the shelf and go on about your business.

On the other hand, if your soul's response is "Well duh," then pay laser beam attention to what I'm about to share with you. We need to talk. One of the ancient Psalmists put it this way: "O God, You have taught me from my earliest childhood, and I have constantly told others about the wonderful things You do. Now that I am old and gray, do not abandon me, O God. Let me proclaim your power to this new generation, your mighty miracles to all who come after me." [2] Mighty miracles are exactly what we are going to pursue.

---

[1] II Cor. 5:17 (NLT).
[2] Psm 71:17-18 (NLT).

If you know little or nothing of spiritual matters or think they are more mythical than real, I don't care, and God isn't worried. If you've been "around God" all your life, but found your experience sadly more talk than action, more just a code of ethics, I have a surprise for you. Although usually subtle, usually quiet but not always, this surprise for you *will* be unmistakable. You will not have to wonder if it is real.

You will not have to go to classes, listen to every form of human waxing ever uttered, or enter a debate; you will not Have to do some type of auto-suggestion to convince yourself-- you will know. It will not matter now how huge your mound of garbage or how little your knowledge. Listen….you do not even have to believe what I'm saying. I kid you NOT. However, if you will stick it out with me, you will concur with one of the greatest of our Christian forefathers who said: "I have discarded *everything* else, counting it all as garbage, so that I may have Christ and become one with Him" [3] Actually, Paul used a much stronger term than "garbage." I really like that guy.

You must achieve only one quality to begin reaping the treasures of what I am about to share with you: you *must* become willing. OK, OK, don't toss this word from your mind like swatting away a mental fly. The decision to become willing, seemingly so simple, may be the critical internal debate of your life to this moment. Our first spiritual **EXPLOSION**: If you cannot honestly and thoroughly be willing, God will *give* willingness to you as a gift.

---

[3] Phil 3: 8-9 (NLT).

What a deal! You just ask for willingness. Repeatedly. If you have no idea whom you are asking, ask the sky; ask Whoever might be *there* – just know it is not you! If you will not, then there you go: you just are not willing. Tragically, that leaves you a member of a very large herd. I love Herbert Spencer's statement found in the "Big Book," <u>Alcoholics Anonymous</u>: "There is a principle which is a bar against all information, which is proof against all arguments and which cannot fail to keep a man in everlasting ignorance—that principal is contempt prior to investigation." If you are a proud member of this mindset, I am crushed for you.

Now am I saying that when you close the cover on this book, your life will be magically changed into bliss and ease? Of course not. You have lived a long time learning to live your life, and God has no desire to be your genie. Things have happened that cannot un-happen. Some were your fault, some were just tragedies that befell you. You could not be an adult the day you arrived. What I *am* telling you is that this book can be your manufacturer's handbook, a map that will lead you into the Kingdom of God.

You will not have to ask yourself and others anymore, "Where's the Beef?" You will not have to continue wandering around in the wilderness, wondering, wishing and hoping that the Kingdom is real. If you will commit to a process that I am going to describe, accept it (that's important…your choice: to accept) and simply open yourself to whatever Force there may be that wants to woo you and intervene in your life, everything about you is going to be different….dramatically different…. and you will know it. You will know it!!

CHAPTER TWO

"Bennett, are you a Kook?"

You may be asking where I get off making such claims, offering such hope. I am not a guru. I am not an extraordinary person. I am not a theologian, a minister, a Bible scholar, or a sage. I have never been to seminary. I am a sixty- nine year old, one-man shop real estate guy in the poorest of these United States. I have never written a book.

I have resisted for several reasons. First, I am terrified of my pride. I am reluctant to be vulnerable to whatever small recognition might come to me, even if nobody reads this but my family and a few friends. I am also scared of absolute failure.... what if those closest to me are not even receptive to the Truth offered here? What slim chance might there be that this book will ever in any way be distributed? Whatever response might follow, my ego is one of my most dangerous defects.

Secondly, what am I to say? What have I to offer? Who will care? There are millions of books about "religion." All I know is what I know, what has happened to me. Lastly, there's the fraud factor. I am presenting myself in one light when I am actually a double agent. I have a dark side. Although I know I am worthy in my God's eyes because of our relationship and I know what He has done for me, I see my dark side and am aghast. Then I am reminded that God has always loved it when the fallen allow themselves to be clay in his hands.

In my observation of the early faith pioneers, I sense they were minding their own business with not a thought of leading, witnessing, or even working for a higher purpose. They mostly did not even volunteer. They were just doing their deal and suddenly God stopped by. They were chosen, commanded, lifted. I have not experienced that in any profound way; I have only felt nudges, but those nudges have become more pronounced through the years.

I've learned, however, that when the whispers continue, I am expected to listen and then act. God hands out various gifts to each one of us. I have the ability to communicate my experience. I believe He has given that gift to me with something in mind. So, here I am, compelled to share my discoveries with you.

These experiences I will be sharing with you are partly what has happened to me and partly what I have observed in many, many others. I believe God wants me to tell you my story, His story. He has hit the ball into my court; I simply have to swing at it. My part is to suit up, show up, tell the truth, and not be attached to the outcome. [4] God's part is what is going to *happen to you.*

---

[4] A quip from Rev. Edwin Bacon.

Perhaps it *is* because I am so ordinary that He whispers to me. He absolutely adores ordinary, whupped down, wormy-weak people. I know this. I know it. You are going to know it too. We are going to be talking about only what can be known and experienced. Nothing theoretical. We are going to be talking about and laying hold of Power. You will not just be hearing about it. If you are like me, you have had an ample supply of talk. So hang in, my wormy-weak [5] or my cynically-sad friend.

EXPLOSION: (Whether you agree with secrets I describe as explosions doesn't matter – they are.) Timing in spiritual matters is often a conundrum. (Why else are we just now talking?) DO NOT GIVE UP BEFORE THE MIRACLE HAPPENS! Yes, highlight that sentence and come back to it over and over. It is a cornerstone for what we are going to experience. Notice, I did not say discuss; I said experience.

My God is not into pabulum. He is not into endless, fruitless talk. He is into Life; He is into action; He is into power. If you will become willing, God is going to change everything about you. Notice I did not say if you "can" become willing. This is not a matter of can or can't. Stop fooling yourself. Oh, I did that for years! It is this simple: it is a matter of will or won't. God is waiting. He has been waiting. He is excited!

---

[5] In Psa 22, David said, "I am a worm and not a man." (NLT). It must have been one of Jesus' "go to" psalms because it seems to describe the crucifixion torture He eventually endured and He quoted its opening lines on the Cross.

CHAPTER THREE

Refusing a Royal Invitation

Now there *is* some bad news: since the beginning of time, people have refused to engage Him, even during desperate times. It is not any different now. Many people are like clams, as one of my meditations describes, lying on the bottom of the ocean, thinking they know about the world and its workings but imprisoned by their hard shells of indifference and unwillingness.[6] The life and death truth is this: now, as we think and pray together, you will have to slink away to remain the same. Ka-POW!

EXPLOSION: (I know they are coming fast!) The natural law is this: I will not commit to something I do not understand. I am just not into mysteries and miracles. On the other hand, God makes the spiritual law clear. He says, "I am asking you to commit now, without your usual requirements, and I will give you understanding as you are able to receive it." [7] That

---

[6] <u>Streams in the Desert</u>, L.B. Coman.
[7] John 7:17, 14:21, 8:31-32, Rom 12:2.

is simply His rule. You *must* be willing to try if you want to win the Prize. And what is the Prize? A new love, a new romance, a new courtship, a new confidence, a new Life, a new everything! I would like to actually touch Peace and Joy. Find them. Hold them. Live them. Wouldn't you?

If you stay with me, if you become willing, if you commit to the process, you will look back at some point and know that this decision was a pivotal moment in your life. Not because of me. I am about as average a skinny legged, balding, below-the-radar-type guy as you can imagine. I tote a train load of baggage. But I know something which I have found through years of some pain and desperation.

EXPLOSION: The saving Secret that will transform you is all the more powerful upon a complete and absolute demolishment of your life. If you are a desperado, move to the front of the starting line. Do NOT despise your pathetic state any longer….it is meant to be what Frederick Buechner has called a fearsome blessing! I think God jumps for joy at us desperadoes. We are finally broken within ourselves.

This something I know is actually Someone. I do not just know about Him, I know Him… intimately. That is not a merit badge. I am a noodle… but listen: I have received a free gift, and I am going to reveal to you how you may receive it as well. If you become willing, and if you join me in the pilgrimage I describe, you also *WILL* receive this indescribable gift. By the way, I didn't become willing easily either! Becoming willing for me was like trying to give a tub–bath to a feral cat! This gift is the reason He dreamed of you and gave you life. The gift is yours already. However, many of us have simply not known how to unwrap it. Somehow we have not received the notice… but that is about to change…. if you are willing!

Now, we need to get this straight from the beginning. I am a Christian. Everything I have learned from God is through this mystery called the Holy Trinity. You do not have to know history as God has developed it; it is far more wonderful to know Him! But the truth is, God created all, just as He said. He and His Son and His Holy Spirit were all together from the beginning. When He decided the time was right, God disguised Himself and joined us as a baby…then a man…to save us from ourselves.

Why do we need saving? It is because we are spiritual beings designed for a love affair with the One who gave us life. However, because we are living for only a moment in natural bodies, and because He wanted us to have the freedom to live with and in Him or to refuse Him; we veer toward becoming fools because we do not understand. I read recently a Flannery O'Connor quip: "It does not take much to make us realize what fools we are, but the little it takes is so long in coming. I see my ridiculous self by degrees." [8]

Oh man, I wish I'd said that…it is my story! Now back to my point: we live for self, and that causes death… death to our souls and death to our lives. This is sin at its basic root. The Holy Trinity allow*ed us to* be this way. **EXPLOSION:** God designed us this way from the beginning of time to feel an emptiness without His presence in our lives. So, this enigmatic Trinity--God the Father, God the Son, and God the Holy

---
[8] <u>Prayer: Experiencing Awe and Intimacy with God</u> Timothy Keller.

Ghost—designed the remedy. You do not have to agree with me at this moment. I just need for you to know where I am coming from—Truth as I receive it—which leads to another **EXPLOSION:** Truth can be known—revealed and grasped for dear Life.

Know this: God longs to bring you into a knowledge of and an intimacy with Him; He uses the image that we and He become one.[9] *Very intimate,* is it not? He wants to show you this Truth. You may not care, you may not believe it, and you may or may not wish that it were so.

Something else about Him: He loves using plain folks to tell this Truth. I'm about as "plain folks" as you can get. I'm just a man, no different from you. But I know what I know. With all my limitations and emotional deformities (and folks, I will tell you the truth—mine are size XXXL) and with His Power manifested through my weakness, I trust Him to touch *you.* He has *chosen* you.[10]

You are not reading this humble book by happenstance. Whether you believe that or not, again, that does not matter. You are being invited to leave luke warmness, emptiness, confusion, doubt, and/or indifference far behind. Whether or not you will become willing…this is a turning-point choice of your life. If you have read this far in this book and still feel unwilling, ask God for willingness. Now! Repeatedly! Like Your life depends on it. Not because *He* has to be reminded that we want willingness. **We need to be reminded.**

---

[9] John 17:21 (NLT).

[10] John 15:16 (NLT).

CHAPTER FOUR

So Where Do We Start?

Yes, where do I start? Lord, help me!! Let's start with the basics. Let's talk about what nobody talks about. That should be the place if it is a basic, should it not? Let's start with sin. Did your heart sink? Did your eyes roll? I know, I know… not the most comfortable start. We have to address it. Why? Our sin is what blocks our Spirit from our Creator. We *must* see and address the blocks, or we are just boxing the wind and NOTHING will change! [11]

I love stories. Let me share with you a true experience. My long-time friend Dan, who is more like my brother, and I were mentoring fifth and sixth graders in a low-income neighborhood school. Dan was working with little Johnny. Our routine was that once a week we would stop by a fast food place, pick up burgers and soda, and get the kids out of the cafeteria for a private lunch in a quiet spot.

---

[11] Rom 2:1, 1st John 2: 3-6.

The aim was to try to establish a relationship so that we could be of some help to the kids…mostly encourage them, hear their struggles, and be their friend. We hoped that these beginnings would lead to outside school activities: going to a movie, taking them camping or fishing, or just tossing a football on the playground. We hoped that spiritual lessons would become part of the conversation. If the children would allow us into their lives, we could encourage them through high school and on to whatever lay beyond.

This particular day, Dan was in his law firm office for an important meeting when he suddenly remembered he had a lunch appointment with Johnny. In a frenzy, he rushed to pick up the burgers and fries and raced to the school. Out of breath, stressed, but anxious to love this little boy, he spread out the grub of choice between them. "How's it going, Johnny?" he asked. Silence. Johnny didn't eat. He stared at his shoes. "Do you not like hamburgers and fries? Are you not hungry?" Johnny gave a barely audible groan. He kept his eyes on the floor. "Would you like me to bring something different next Friday, Johnny?" "Naw." They sat in silence for a few minutes,

Dan was becoming more and more frustrated and the little boy was still avoiding his eyes. Finally Johnny whispered, "I wanna go back." He staggered up and slumped out of the room. Dan slammed the food into the garbage, stormed back to his car, and started back downtown.

Dan began to file his complaint. "Lord," he said, "what am I to do? I busted my rear leaving a meeting to get over there, and I know I can help him…I know I could make his life better… but he won't even look up. How can I get through to him, to let him know I care, that I'm here for him? I'm about ready to chuck this, Lord!" There was silence in the car. Then Dan heard the whisper; "I know exactly how you feel. I know exactly how it goes. Remember, I'm a mentor too....yours."

Oh, what a round-house slobber-clobber! I have been little Johnny so many years while I was ignoring, insulting, minimalizing, and treating my God as unworthy of my smallest response. I rebuffed His every approach.

Another story. In 1968, I was driving my Volkswagen Bug to work one morning in our small southern city, listening to Farmer Jim Neal's talk show on the radio. Farmer Jim and his "Feist Dog" were a legendary team of homespun humor and wisdom. Jim was drawling along when my ears perked up. "All ya'll in the class of '48 over at Central High are invited to your Twenty-year class reunion this Saturday night at the Robert E. Lee Hotel. Now don't you dare miss this. All your classmates just can't WAIT to see how bad you done messed up." Well, I laughed out loud. That was then. Years later, as life failed to be the Big Top Parade I had planned, that memory somehow became less humorous.

Let me tell you what I finally began to comprehend after so long. **EXPLOSION:** The reason my life seemed to be flipping and flopping like a fish on a pier was that sin was mauling me. I had been absolutely unaware of my problem. I considered myself a good person who'd had a streak of bad luck. I thought endurance and darkness were all my life was meant to be with whatever globs of "ease" I could grab as my train jolted along.

As stated earlier, gradually in my journey I discovered that the essence of sin is promotion of self and that God has laid down a law regarding that sin: His law states that we cannot serve two masters, or put another way; a house divided cannot stand. Check it out in Matt 12; 25 and Mark 3:25. You may rest assured this law will not be adjusted in relation to culture, circumstances, or time. I spent a lifetime with no understanding of this law. Most of us have operated on the premise that we do not murder, do not rob, do not commit adultery, and do not cheat on our taxes, maybe we rarely even lie.

Congratulations. We feel pretty good about our basic goodness. I did. What has been the purpose of our lives? Forget goals. That's different. What has been your purpose? Consider this question with life-threatening seriousness. Have we not all operated mostly in the domain of self- propulsion?[12] Haven't our lives been oriented to promotion and protection of ole number one? It's human nature. The problem is, as mentioned earlier, we are spiritual beings. Our human being phase is strictly a moment in time; we are designed and created for Eternity where God's "All-ness" will be all!

So let's ask the in-vogue question: this constant striving for self enhancement – how's that workin' out for ya? We have already gotten honest and admitted something is off kilter in our lives. We feel as if some parts are missing. The scale ranges from a misty lost-ness to desperate pain. What we have failed to grasp is that as long as our wills are tuned to satisfy ourselves, we have a tendency to stagger and stumble. Many of us have made a complete mess of things. Others just sense this vague voice that asks "is this all there is?" We find

---

[12] I love this phrase from the "Big Book," Alcoholics Anonymous.

So Where Do We Start?

ourselves grappling with shame, resentment, anger, dishonesty, fear, insecurities, broken relationships with others and with ourselves. These emotional and spiritual deformities steal our energy and much of our focus and become walls between us and God. Make no mistake—God doesn't fool around. He calls these defects Idols, and He is jealous of them.[13]

We may not realize their toxicity, but that is precisely the problem. God takes them seriously because He knows that they are spiritual and emotional cancers. It took me a lifetime to discover what would appear to be spiritually elemental. **EXPLOSION:** These self-gods are what make our lives miserable! THAT is why God hates them. Their rewards are loneliness, fear, anxiety, pain, sorrow, resentments, despair, self-pity, and a hump-back heavy with additional emotional anvils.

So things haven't worked out so well. The truth is, our self-reliance has not been enough. We find ourselves broken, wounded. Now if doing things *our way* has not worked out as well as we had hoped, what do you think that suggests? Might we venture a test? You know what? Our culture has too long preached a withered gospel of ideas and concepts. The problem is that that gospel has been powerless to change us. It has had little or no transformational qualities. There is no power! So what gives? Jesus' earliest message was "Repent!"[14] What did He mean? He added that the Kingdom of God was near. Hmmm. "Thy Kingdom come, Thy will be done....Repent."

---

[13] Exodus 20:3.
[14] Mark 1:15, Matt 4:17.

Sounds like God was anticipating a real change. Have you changed spiritually in the past year, two years, five years? If you don't know….what does that mean? It sounds as if He *expects* us to become *different.* It sounds as if there should be an action, and then a result. How could I have missed this *requirement* all these years? Let us ponder doing something radical, something different. What if we come to our senses and see that all our best efforts and smartest thoughts have not brought us within sight of this mysterious "Kingdom." What do you suppose we might try? How about obedience?

Bingo! I came to the same conclusion.

If what we are doing is not working, why not just take the *Holy Hint*, and *make a decision to surrender* to His will and do it? What do we have to lose? What if He is telling us the Truth, and we've been too blind, too self- absorbed, and too stubborn to try it? Why not put this "Truth" to the test? I mean all we are talking about here is quality of life. New Life! All we are talking about is the possibility of lining ourselves up with the One who adores us, who created us through His perfect planning, and who wants to give us Life in its Fullness. That is what He has told us.[15] I am not making this stuff up!

---

[15] John 3:16, 10:10, Psa 139:13-16.

CHAPTER FIVE

Half Way There Is Not There

Have you ever wondered why you have never met or heard of anyone who was like Peter, James, and John? They were Saints who, while being humble men from a po-dunk area of the Roman Empire, changed the world by a power they had no reason to possess. Well, we're going to investigate that, but I submit to you that one reason is that you and I do not *know* anyone who wants to and actually does live a life absolutely surrendered to Jesus, the Christ; who wants to expand the Kingdom of God with *nothing* else in competition. Well I know some ministers who, I believe, seek to live a life of total surrender, but nobody like you and me. We have no thought of doing such a thing. Why, it never even occurred to me! I am not talking about a new career or in some way lessoning our devotion to our loved ones. I *am* talking about Life Purpose.

Jesus said in Matthew 5, "Blessed are the pure in heart." We have heard that scripture all our lives, but what did Jesus mean? I believe part of what He meant was an undivided heart.

I have found that this is *precisely* where I get lost. Our wills are divided – our hearts are divided. **EXPLOSION:** If one's will partly does things God's way, but the other part does things our way, spiritual and moral confusion are the *inevitable* result. Mark that word: *Inevitable!* Would you agree? How could one have peace during a tug of war for our souls that is the result of a half measure of will? If you were having a love affair with two people at once, trying to balance between your first love and then your second, the result is predictable: you cannot love either with all your heart; neither of them can have all of you!

We pass through this temporal world, but whether we know it or not, we belong to Heaven. This conflict begets our predicament, and we know not what to do. But we do! That is exactly what this book is about. God does not leave us as orphans. (He actually said that!) [16] **EXPLOSION:** We make a *decision*. We decide that the wisest and most profitable, the most self-honoring and most healing thing to do is to start trying to find His will for us and then do it. Doing things our way has brought us either no awareness of a nearby Kingdom of Glory or disappointment in various forms.

EXPLOSION: Have you ever examined your fear, loneliness, anger, resentment, or dishonesty? If you look carefully at your pain, you will find that you are resisting something that you believe threatens self. Does it not have to do with something you want, or something you might lose? Ah Ha! *The pain is in the resistance!* What if we decided to change this strategy of self- protection and self- promotion? What if we

---

[16] John 14:18.

simply decided to try it His way? Do you know you will have just considered making one of the most radical decisions of your life? We are joining the Psalmist who cried out, "O LORD, give me an undivided heart!"[17]

So, how do I acquire an undivided heart? I'm soooo glad you asked that! Your part is surprisingly simple. You have made a decision to change your mind. That is what our God describes as repentance—the desire first, and then the decision to change course – to act! Did you know that God will give you the tools to draw nearer to Him if you want to? He is *already* near you. He is waiting!

EXPLOSION: There lies a gem. It is right there in our "want to," which leads to a back-to-back **EXPLOSION:** You can have *all of God you want.* So our "want to" factor has been lacking. It sounds almost too simple...but have we not lived our lives thus far wandering along not comprehending this elementary Truth? The more deeply we want to find God, the more the path opens. I couldn't make this stuff up. I am quoting none other than the Alpha and the Omega: "if you seek Me, with ALL your heart, you WILL find Me." [18]

This truth is another spiritual law that seems to have gotten misplaced. We are going to talk a great deal about these Truths. We are going to grab hold of them, surrender to them, and then we are going to discover A Great Secret. *Something un-dang-imaginable is going to happen!!*

---

[17] Psa 86:11.
[18] Deut 4:29, Jer 29:13, Luke 11:9-10, Matt 7:7, 8.

CHAPTER SIX

Getting Serious for the First Time

Now remember when we started our discussion about sin, we started with the suspicion that "there might be something in me that is blocking me from God." Let's get serious. No more talk. Let's walk. Stop: get a pad and pen. Find a quiet place and time. No interruptions. I want you to write down every negative thought or experience in your memory. Do not allow yourself to think of anyone else to blame. Do not allow any victimhood to intrude into your examination. I want you to be ruthlessly honest with yourself.

Write down what hurt you as a child and throughout your life, what your fears are, what angers you have, what resentments, what wrongs you've done to others or yourself. Write down what you think could be blocks, idols, or even addictions: alcohol or drugs, certainly. What about people – your children, your friends; what about control, what about fear, what about greed, what about ambition, prestige, intellect, perfection, reputation. What about religion and church; what about vanity, what about career, what about busyness, what about hobbies?

Befuzzled? Check out your check stubs. Do you think you could be addicted to yourself? Could self- centeredness be an addiction? Consider hobbies, sex, food, tech gadgets, etc. You and I know people who are addicted to misery—victimhood, suffering, and crisis! Let's define an idol as something you do with more energy, more time and focus than you give to God. "Whew…Bennett…surely you aren't serious?" God is extremely serious.

What regrets do you have? Once again, whom have you hurt? Forget what they did. For these purposes, it doesn't matter. If you have not identified some problems with the above suggestions, maybe you have one of my addictions, one of my favorites: denial. Melody Beattie in <u>The Language of Letting Go</u> describes denial as the shock absorber of the soul. Start again and be unflinchingly honest. If you see yourself more clearly, welcome to the human condition!

Now I want you to notice whether your spirit resists this self- exam! Notice your heart: is it offended? Is someone or something whispering to you, "Oh…I remember this hell-fire and damnation stuff; this is that old beat- yourself- up and take a guilt trip routine?" It is fear- based religion. God does not want that. He loves me! He has forgiven me! My passport is stamped! Child of God…do not buy it. Look where that old thought exercise has landed you! Of course God loves you! He adores you. That is why He is speaking to you now. He has a better life for you, but He has laid down another spiritual law.

EXPLOSION: God measures our love by our obedience. He repeatedly says; "The ones who love Me are the ones who obey Me."[19] Why do you think people resist God? I think it has to do with our repulsion to obedience.[20] We resist every type of submission. Have we not made idols of ourselves? I am here to tell you, shout to you, that these precise thoughts, this dismissing of radical obedience, will keep you in a web of emptiness, in your self- made fog of "is this all," and you will remain a wanderer in a wilderness; your spiritual experience will continue to resemble milquetoast! How do I know these things? Because I was a slave to independence for YEARS! I'm STILL stepping through the mess! In spiritual matters, independence is the Big Lie!

Did you write your stuff down? If you did not, what do you think that says about your willingness factor? Please, please, pray more for willingness. Because...this is vital, beloved of God; if nothing changes, nothing changes. My wife reminds me often: "If the pain of not changing is not greater than the pain of changing, nothing is going to happen. (She is one of the most wonderful blessings God has given me! She is *very* wise!)

We are searching for the Kingdom of God! This is our life! We *must* make some changes (repent). Only then will we find the pathways that have heretofore been hidden. *Do not* let this become just another book that goes onto the stack when and if you can finish. If we stay in denial of the blocks and *refuse to* make changes, our chances are, frankly, slim. We are praying

---

[19] John 14:15, 21, 23-24, John 4:34, Luke 6:46-49.
[20] John 3:20.

Getting Serious for the First Time

for an undivided will! Remember what we said a few moments ago: the pain is the result of resisting! Mine as well as yours!

We are searching for the new path…the one where self becomes smaller and He becomes larger! If we were dead to self, there would be a lot less pain. Several times in Scripture, Jesus wraps Truth in paradox: "You must lose your life in order to find it."[21] Is He talking in riddles or is He speaking a monumental Truth? For the moment, fold your list, put it somewhere where no one will find it, but do not scrap it. We're coming back to it.

We *must* discover the way to the Spiritual realm in order to experience knowable transformation. We can and we will, and we can start now. Amazing developments are coming! Listen… we will never be given absolute clarity. Clarity can easily become an idol. God does not explain all to us. Jesus states again and again, "Just trust Me." The natural law teaches to commit only when we understand.

EXPLOSION: The Spiritual Law is God saying, "Commit first, and I will give you understanding as you are ready to receive."[22] This goes slam-up against every fiber of our being. The astounding news is He has been waiting… **EXPLOSION:** He is *planning* to help us! Remember when He turned to a couple of guys who were timidly trailing him for the first time, and who were wondering if this strange Man could really be Something Special? Remember how he answered them? "Come and see!"[23]

Let's do it!

---

[21] John 12:24-25, Mark 8:34-35.

[22] John 7:17, 8:31, 14:21, 16:12-13, 25.

[23] John 1:37-39.

CHAPTER SEVEN

Cotton Candy

We need to stop here – take Intermission somewhat ahead of time and consider a fork in our path. Christianity teaches that we are saved by Faith and Faith alone, i.e., by simply confessing that Jesus is Lord and believing He is who He says He is, our entry to Everlasting Life with God is accomplished.[24] What about now…doesn't He claim to be Something Spectacular for us now?

For much of my life, I stamped my passport with the above acquiescence and toodled not-so–merrily on my way. I greatly enjoyed my cotton candy gospel. Basking in God's love and mercy was pure sugar that melted in my mouth. However, I was receiving no nutrients, no nourishment! I kept growing weaker. The blade of my spiritual "knife" became more and more dull as my life continued to gradually unravel. I stumbled along, groping, grabbing, and grubbing for life, becoming more

---
[24] Acts 16:30-31, John 3:16, 6:28-29, 14:11, Gal 3:9, Eph 1:8, Phil 3:9.

and more isolated from something, but I knew not what. "I am a Christian," I told myself. "Where is God? Is this thing I attend once a week just a Sunday civic group meeting? We sing, we pray, we hear a nice talk, we plan some service work, we form some committees, we pay the dues, and we go home."

I had held fast to this soft and mellow gospel when the Truth was that God desired more of me than I had been willing to give, and I had no idea what was wrong. If I had taken the time to investigate, I would have found that God was calling me to trust Him with every portion of my life, to let nothing stand ahead of Him or between us. NOTHING! I also would have found that it has been this way…people refusing Him in overt and covert rebellion…since the beginning of time.[25]

God loves you and me. It is true we are saved by faith. Through this faith we are "in Christ" because the Father deemed it so, and we possess through His Grace the third person of the Trinity, The Holy Spirit. But these things are too often a conundrum to us. Does anything different happen to us?

Faith is not just admitting that God exists. God speaks through His Holy Scriptures, and He says time and time again: this is about surrender; this is about your heart; this is about becoming someone new…someone vastly different from who you have been. This is about allowing the Holy Spirit to be activated in your heart. This is about repentance, and repentance means CHANGE! Ambling along, unmoved by His voice, His presence, His wooing, changes NOTHING! If you and I are not changing…. if we are quite unaware that changes are

---

[25] John 3:18-21, 8:42-47, Acts 7:51-53, Rom 1:18-25.

happening in our natural and spiritual lives, I would submit to you that the diagnosis is "no change." Something is very wrong; something is missing.

So listen, beloved of God, and that is miraculously who you are. What we are talking about now is becoming receptive to and desiring change. You do not have to understand what change might have to happen or how it might be made to happen. What is important is that you understand you and I are no longer going to be resting under the illusion of our stamped passport while we continue to live lives that separate us from something vital, something so wonderful that as we gradually make our discovery we will begin to identify with Paul when he said that everything that came before THIS was pure manure!"[26]

End of Intermission. Let us now get to the good stuff!!

---

[26] Phil 3:7-8.

CHAPTER EIGHT

The Secret

I suspect I know what you are thinking. You are saying to yourself, "Yeah, I would love to find this Life Bennett describes, but I know myself. I have read a hundred self-help books. I have read sevendyleven religious gurus. I have gone to retreats and seminars. I have done all I could to improve myself, to change. If I am truthful, I know deep down, I will not be any different after reading all this…even with becoming willing to change. I will not. And I sense that familiar, thinly disguised depression because…I really want to find my Life…the one my Creator had in mind for me….if it is really there and different from the one I have had."

Beloved of God: of course you can't do this. I know what you know because I have been right there in the boat with you. You and I are utterly helpless to make anything but temporary, elusive attempts. After a short period of well-intentioned work and determination, we have always returned to our well-worn, same selves. The book gets tossed, the week-end retreat forgotten, the lingering regret seeps back like a flood slowly slipping under the house door. Our lives of "quiet desperation" set back in and we trudge on, squashing our disappointment into the lower levels of our consciousness. Survival, we decide, is the best we can realize; endure, buck up, hope there is an after- life and it will be better. What we are left with is feeling spiritually adrift, spiritually hopeless, on our own.

Let's be honest and admit it: we are powerless. "Bennett, you are asking me to change my heart. You are expecting me to become someone I am not…and I cannot change myself. I have tried this before. You might as well ask me to grow another arm. I am who I am. So…all this is not for me. Whatever it is… do not flim- flam me with promises of joy, peace, and a better life. I have been disappointed too many times already!"

Do you think God does not know your every thought, every feeling, and every word? Of course He does. He knows you better than YOU know you. He has known everything all along![27] So open your heart, crank up your willingness, and receive and embrace what I am going to tell you now as the most life changing discovery of your life.

Do you remember – and if you do not, you can look it up later—during the last days before Jesus was crucified, He was spending some special teaching moments with His disciples, well aware that His time was very short? He was preparing them. He was depending upon them to change the entire world, forever. They were a seemingly motley crew – not sophisticated, nor educated, nor influential, nor wealthy. This is the

---

[27] Psa 139:1-5 (NLT).

traditional thought, but can you tell me Peter, James, and John were not extraordinary? They may have been country boys, but they were way ahead in heart. Although they had no social standing, were not the clergy, and had no political power, they were His chosen, His choice—average, everyday folk…like US!

They were all-in and anxious to prove their love and devotion to Jesus. They knew Him better than anyone on earth. They sat at His table, watched Him preach and teach, witnessed uncountable miracles, and talked hours upon hours with Him every day and night for three years! They were absolutely "pure in heart." They KNEW who He was, and they had no other agenda in their lives except to follow Him. They were prepared with all the knowledge, all the conviction, all the passion they would need. They were ready for whatever was to come. Well, at least, that was what they assured Him. (It's all in John's gospel.) Jesus had carefully brought them along, slowly, patiently, tenderly – teaching them, loving them, revealing the very Kingdom of God to them. He gave them the new command to love others, just as He had loved them.[28] It was an extraordinary moment in history, a glorious moment for mankind.

Jesus then dropped another **EXPLOSION** the disciples hand not fully grasped: He was leaving them. They were to carry on everything He had taught them. They were crushed and bewildered, but He told them something mysterious was coming. He told them it was actually best that He leave them because He was going to send them a new Helper, a

---

[28] John 13:34 (NLT).

Counselor. He told them this Helper would be their guide, that He, the Helper, would relay instructions to them directly from Jesus. This Counselor would tell them even more than Jesus had been able to tell them in these short years.

He told them that it would be through this Helper that they would become one with Him and the Father, that somehow *God Himself would enter their spirits and they would become one!* He prayed for them, and in that prayer He also prayed for us:"I am praying not only for these disciples but also for *all who will ever believe in me because of their testimony."* He not only wanted them to receive all that He had for them, but He also planned for us to receive it as well. Everything He offered to them, He was offering to us![29] Just a few hours later the world apparently lost all as Jesus, The Prince of Peace and the King of Glory, was tortured to death.

You know what happened. God raised His Son from that death, and the disciples, at first disbelieving, were thrilled beyond imagining. Now they were walking on air…their lives forever new, full of excitement and confidence and bursting to shout to the world what they had witnessed. For the moment, He was BACK! All that talk about a Helper was forgotten. Their King of Glory made seemingly random appearances to various individuals and groups. Now here is where the story becomes even more astounding. It is here that many people of faith seem to have missed something absolutely strategic and vital. Jesus meets his innermost group again…the last time they see Him. He utters His final, never-to-be-forgotten words: "Do not

---

[29] "Breaking News, today!" John 14-17.

leave Jerusalem until the Father sends you what He promised. Remember, I have told you about this before. John baptized with water, but in just a few days you will be baptized with the Holy Spirit."[30]

Whoa...here were his hand-selected charges....bursting with affection and knowledge....and yet....they were told not to go. What? What? Why? Why didn't Jesus do what any commander would do after all the training and teaching and conditioning were complete? Why didn't He say, "Ok, troops, move out!" But...they *were not* ready. They didn't know it, but something was lacking. Something critical. They were just normal people who were being called on to spark a spiritual revolution. They needed something MORE. So they were ordered to wait... wait for something that would come to them just as Jesus had promised. They needed supernatural qualities!!

Dear beloved of God, *Jesus knew His disciples were utterly incapable of doing what He was asking them to do if all they had was themselves to do it. They were to wait until they were equipped as a result of receiving His Holy Spirit power ... a power from God that would enable them to do what they absolutely could not have done , a power that would make them different people!!*

Just days later, these same simple folk were gathered together when the Spirit "fell" upon them. It was an earthquake moment. You can read about it in Acts II. *This* was the beginning of a new era in God's history. No more did His Spirit come to just a few individuals here and there for special ministry as

---

[30] Acts 1:4-5 (NLT).

He had done with the great prophets and leaders of the Old Testament. God had foretold a time when His Spirit would be poured out on all people, remaking men's hearts, and this was the inaugural celebration.[31]

This was the beginning of what John the Baptist had described when he told the people in the wilderness that while he baptized with water, someone was coming who would baptize them with fire and the Holy Spirit.[32] The group gathered that day saw visions of fire as they began to think differently, feel differently, to understand differently, to see a way to live life differently. Receiving the Person of the Holy Spirit was the fulfillment of what Jesus had told the disciples during His final days on earth. **EXPLOSION:** *We can choose to receive the Holy Spirit. It is a living part of the Gospel and designed for empowering us today!* No wonder we are powerless to become who He calls us to be! He knew we would be! We do *not* have the power. He *does* have the power, and **EXPLOSION:** He wants to give it to us!

Now, it is critical for us to understand something. We are not talking about becoming super people, but supernatural people. *This phenomenon has always been hard to grasp!* Even from the start. Even when Peter was calling for change, telling everyone he could get to listen, "Each of you must turn from your former selves, look to God, and be baptized in the name of Jesus Christ for the forgiveness of your sins. *Then*

---

[31] Ex 36:25-27, Isaiah 43:18-20, 59:20-21, Eze 11:19-20, 36:25-27, Joel 3:28-29, Heb 8:6-13.

[32] Matt 3:11, Mark 1:7-8, Luke 3:16, John 1:33-34.

you will receive the gift of the Holy Spirit. This promise is to you and your children, and even to the Gentiles (non- Jews), all who have been called by the Lord our God!"[33]

Oh..... Oh, we have such trouble grasping this Truth! We can conceive of and welcome the part about forgiveness, but the promise of the Holy Spirit is so often an enigma. Because we do not understand; we refuse to open our hearts and receive. Look what was happening even then. One of these early guys, Stephen, was stoned for daring to say: "You stubborn people! You are heathen at heart and deaf to the truth. Must you forever resist the Holy Spirit?"[34]

A short time later, the disciples in Jerusalem heard that some Samaritans believed this new gospel message, so Peter and John rushed to reinforce it. When they arrived, they realized these folk had already been baptized in Jesus' name, but *they had not yet received the Holy Spirit!* Peter and John were aghast. "You are missing the most wonderful part!" They immediately prayed for these new believers to receive this additional power.[35]

EXPLOSION: God also *does* love to use the best and brightest folk, even when they have not been listening. I mentioned to you earlier about this fellow Paul...the guy was a big-time Jew, BIG TIME, persecuting the new Christians, throwing them in jail, or simply having them killed. The Lord had planned to appoint Paul as His special witness to non-Jews (Jesus and

---

[33] Acts 2:38-39 (NLT).

[34] Acts 7:51 (NLT).

[35] Act 8:14-17.

most of his small group were Jews), but first He had to get the man's attention. Paul found himself suddenly knocked off his horse and blind. It is a fascinating story, but the gist of it is that before Paul could even begin the work he had been called by God to do, the Lord sent a man named Ananias to visit Paul to pray for him to receive *the Holy Spirit.* In this case, this Baptism of the Holy Spirit came first, then the water baptism.[36]

Later, Peter was sent to tell the new story to some non-Jews at Caesarea, and before he could even start his teaching, **BAM**...the Holy Spirit came upon them.[37] Even with these experiences, just as Stephen said, the Holy Spirit often was minimized or resisted. Paul continued his travels and found some new believers in Ephesus. Listen to this conversation:

Paul: "Did you receive the Holy Spirit when you believed?"
People: "No, we don't know what you mean. We haven't even heard that there is a Holy Spirit."
Paul: "Then what baptism did you experience?"
People: "The Baptism of John." (They were speaking about the water baptism proclaimed by John the Baptist.)
Paul: "John's baptism was to demonstrate a desire to turn from sin and turn to God." Then Paul prayed for them and they received the Holy Spirit.[38]

---

[36] Acts 9:1-29.
[37] Acts 10:44-48, 11:15-17.
[38] Acts 19:1-7

Do you see the pattern? Do you see why so many of us today have tried to be what God has called us to be and found it utterly impossible? The Truth is, without receiving the Holy Spirit, the effort was, at best, anemic then, and is certainly still true today. We talk about the Holy Spirit, we confess the Holy Spirit, we even pray to be filled with the Holy Spirit, but so often we are absolutely clueless about appropriating His power. How could we not be? We are just like those believers in Ephesus – nobody *told* us! Maybe the Holy Spirit has been taught, or we may even have received prayer. Even though we have Him through God's great grace, if we do not understand how to receive Him into ourselves, He remains a mystery guest in our home.

    Dear ones, if this is new ground for you, we are at the pivot point of your Life. God *longs* for you to receive His precious gift, the process Jesus described as becoming One with Him and the Father – the *receiving* of the Holy Spirit. He is waiting to change you through a power you do not possess, whereby you will gradually move from doubt to conviction, from talk to experience, from old self to new creation.[39] I am going to pray for you and suggest a prayer model for you to continue to pray. I do not have a magic formula…there isn't one; all we have to do is decide we want to receive Him *and ALL that He wants to give us!* He always comes when prayers are offered and received with expectation.[40] Now! Please, if you can, close the

---

[39] Ezek 36:25-27, Rom 8:2,11,14,2:, 1st Cor 2:12, 2nd Cor 3:8, 16-18, Col 3:10, 2nd Tim 1:6-7, Eph 1:13.

[40] Dan 9:23.

door, and go to your knees right now. If you cannot physically kneel, just be quiet and open a willing heart. We do not need long dissertations of explanation. The early receivers did not have that; we just need to do it!

> *Lord Jesus, You are either Everything or nothing. We know or are coming to know which it is. We come to You as Your perfect creation, wanting all of You we can possibly have. We are dry, Lord, like a stiff sponge. We ask You to flood us now with Your Living Water, Your Holy Spirit! Fill us so full that we cannot hold a drop more! Take our dry bones into Your hands and bring us to Life. Change us...we surrender everything to You; Your will, nothing else. Now, will you Welcome Him saying, I receive You, Holy Spirit, in all Your Fullness, now, this moment, this day, and for the rest of my life. I am becoming someone New! Thank you, Thank you that it is done! Amen.*

Don't move. Rest. Relax. Be expectant of His presence. Take all the time you want.
Let Him hold you. Marinate in His Living Water.
Exalt in His hushed coming in Power.
Thank Him that He is mighty to save and change.
Whisper your complete surrender and welcome Pure Serenity.
Receive the Peace of resting in His arms.

CHAPTER NINE

Now What?

"So Bennett, was I supposed to have had some sort of spiritual experience when we said that prayer?" A demonstration of the Holy Spirit's presence is not uncommon, but I *certainly did not* have that experience. In fact, I felt nothing. I felt as if the prayer had been spoken into space and lost. I myself did not pray. Someone else prayed for me in a somewhat chaotic moment. I don't think it mattered who prayed or what I felt, only that I was willing.

However, subtle signs followed and will follow for you. Let me tell you what to look for and what to expect. Remember when we started, I told you that you would not have to wonder about this experience? You would know. I do not know how God is going to start showing up in your life, but I can promise you this: if you will be watchful, and if you continue to reinforce this receiving of His Spirit on a *daily* basis, things are going to start happening.[41] When I say "reinforce this receiving," the first step is continuing to pray your desire to receive every day. Why? There are four reasons.

First, spiritual growth is much like other growth God has designed; it starts in infancy and gradually grows to maturity and fruit bearing. I do not know where you are in your spiritual growth, but I know both you and I have much maturing still ahead.

Secondly, we talked about taking action to assist real change when we first started this discussion. The one thing NOT to do is just amble on from here not giving a thought to what we have just prayed and not staying spiritually *alert*. We have been in some stage, early or advanced, of spiritual zombie-ism for long enough, and that has been our problem!

Thirdly and most importantly – **EXPLOSION:** the "Sender" of the Spirit, Jesus, told us exactly what to do! He said to keep asking, keep asking.[42] When in doubt, how about we just follow directions?

Lastly, and I do not know why, but as one of my earliest mentors explained, "We leak!"[43] If we ignore or forget what we have prayed, we will look in our spiritual rear view mirror one day soon and wonder what that trail of liquid is behind our ride. If this were not true, why would so many believers who have prayed to receive the Holy Spirit feel their lives are without spiritual power?

---

[41] 1st Cor: 2:12.

[42] Luke 11:9-13.

[43] C. Everett "Terry" Fullam.

EXPLOSION: God says over and over in various ways, "If you seek Me *with all your heart,* YOU WILL FIND ME."[44] What we are doing here is discovering how to *seek, find AND RECEIVE* God, with *ALL our heart!* Somehow many of us slept though that class. Now things are very different. You and I are taking on Holy Spirit Power as a daily regimen. As I pleaded with you in the beginning, **hang on until the miracle happens**.[45] It won't be long before you may borrow our southern slang: "now THAT's what I'm talkin 'bout!"

Now is the time to re-test our willingness quotient, our "want-to." I am going to suggest some spiritual alertness exercises/disciplines. **EXPLOSION:** your *willingness* to do these things will be proportionate to *how dramatically you begin to see God moving in a new way in your life!* Metaphorically, we are going to a spiritual gym. Your new Trainer, The Holy Spirit, is going to take you to new realms of Life, but you *must* show up at the gym! So, "NOW HEAR THIS!"

First and foremost: we just prayed for you to receive the Holy Spirit. I want you to continue that prayer daily. This is crucial! So, your first new ACTION is to pray *on your knees* the moment you get out of bed in the morning and the last thing before you climb in at night! "Oh come ON, Bennett, I am perfectly capable of praying while sitting or lying, or standing." Stop! Listen to yourself! Could that be pure pride talking? Stomp on that snake! We agreed to begin making CHANGES!

---

[44] Deut 4:29, Jer 29:13, Luke 11:9-10, Matt 7, 7-8.

[45] .A plea borrowed from Alcoholics Anonymous.

Why is this kneeling important? I am not sure. Maybe it has to do with humbling ourselves. We are coming into the Presence of the King of Glory. Maybe we simply need to exercise a discipline that is more pronounced, physical. In my case, I am reminded of who needs Whom in this deal. I can only tell you something happens in our souls when we humble ourselves every day.

According to Matthew's recording of what has been described as Jesus' Beatitudes, "God blesses those who realize their need for him, for the Kingdom of Heaven is given to them."[46] There is a connection here. (If you are physically unable to kneel, the Lord certainly knows about it.) Don't use my words, use yours, but the prayer should be simple and straight-forward: "Lord, I want all of You I can have! I need You, Holy Spirit! Please give me more! Have Your way with me this day/night. I want to come closer; I want to be Your person. I want You to order my life! Your will only by Your power only. Thank You. I love You. Amen."

---

[46] Matt 5:3 (NLT).

CHAPTER TEN

Wake Up!

The next step is to begin *watching* for God to move in your life. After Jesus was raised from the dead, He started making surprise appearances. One day, several of the disciples decided to go fishing. They fished hard but had nothing to show for their efforts. Suddenly someone was speaking to them from the shore, asking if they were having any luck. They admitted they were not, and the fellow suggested they drop their nets on the other side of the boat. **Whammo!** They hauled in a boat load of fish. They looked back toward the beach-walker in amazement, and John said, "It is the Lord!"[47]

God will begin to make surprise appearances in your life as well! Remember this phrase and be ready to use it: "It is the Lord!" I don't know how He will show up. I doubt He will be a person shouting at you from the beach. He loves to silently come up close without our knowing, but it will be a Holy

---

[47] John 21:7 (NLT).

Bump and you WILL KNOW. Maybe a problem will suddenly be resolved. Maybe someone will say something that gives you an answer or a new understanding for which you were searching. You might hear something you have heard many times, but suddenly you know in your soul it is the Truth! Maybe you will hear a song that suddenly speaks to you as never before. A relationship might improve that has been painful.

A prayer you have offered may be answered and you no longer can label it coincidence. You will stumble upon something written that suddenly leaps from the page, and you will know it is not an accident. You might experience a glorious profession of nature that touches you as never before. You might receive a sense of calm in the middle of a fear-filled night. You hear a whispered thought of assurance that you have never heard before. Every time it happens, shout to yourself, "It is the Lord!" Shout it out loud. Something mystical happens when you speak Holy Words out loud.

EXPLOSION: Did you know God has used the shouts of His people to bring walls crashing to earth?[48] You are going to find yourself waking up to a spiritual world that heretofore has been hidden. God didn't hide it. **EXPLOSION:** God is *constantly* offering personal contact with you. We have struggled in discovering how to tune our spiritual receivers.

---

[48] Josh 6:5.

CHAPTER ELEVEN

Continuing Walking in the Way

Something else is coming and you will know it! You will discover not just a new "interest" in God, but you will notice the beginning of a real *hunger for God!* This feeling may be gradual, it may not, but if your actions reflect those I have laid before you, an unmistakable transformation is coming. "It is the Lord!"

Let us think more about these "changes," these "actions." Why are they so important? It may be because we have a tendency to resist the Holy Spirit.[49] The early leaders noticed that this tendency was tragically common. Have you noticed it in our culture? Resistance to God is everywhere; spiritual matters are for the naive. We must be aware of this rebellion as we press on!

John's gospel makes clear that Jesus equated our love for Him with *obedience.* Yet, I have heard few sermons on the

---
[49] Acts 7:51-53, 19:9, 22:18, 28:24-27, Rom 1:19-22, 1st Cor 1:18-29, John 3:18-21.

subject of obedience. That is why we *must* focus on repentance. God called us, is calling us to make changes. **EXPLOSION:** We cannot change if we are unaware that we ARE disobedient by inaction. So here we go, doing what we have never known before to do.

CHAPTER TWELVE

Find a Mentor

This faith walk is *designed* to be done in community. Jesus instructed the early guys to always take at least one partner with them. The early church leaders – Peter, James, John, and Paul – took someone with them to minister. They stayed in community, which was crucial.[50] I suspect you have noticed that every discipline I am recommending to you is a vital part of your receiving more Holy Spirit Power and *transformation*. You cannot travel this journey alone. I repeat, in matters spiritual, independence is one of the big *lies.* Your next *action-step* is to search for a mentor. If you want to become intimate with God, spend time with someone who is intimate with God. How, you ask? Pray. In your daily prayers, ask God to lead you to someone of His choosing. Then be alert. Watch for someone you know is serious about his or her faith. Then be ready to ask this question when the time is appropriate:

---

[50] Mark 6:7, Acts 1:14, 3:44, Matt 18:20.

"Have you ever had a life-transforming experience through the power of the Holy Spirit?"

If the answer is yes, *you will know it!* You will know it because *the person* will know it. You will observe a sense of urgency in the response. It will be specific. I don't mean in dates or moments, I mean experiences. The answer will exhibit excitement, passion, and *conviction.* A vague answer suggests that this person has not had this experience and therefore cannot convey it.

If you are satisfied with the response, inquire about the source of this person's spiritual nourishment. The answer may or may not be a church. It may be a small group, but wherever it is, ask if you can tag along. If this just is not practical, at the least, ask for recommendations. If you feel comfortable with this person, and the answers given encourage you, be bold! Ask him or her to be your companion as you begin this journey. Explain that you are searching for someone to help you.

You will be surprised how eager Spirit-led Christians are to share what they have discovered!

Your mentor may be a small group. That is what happened to my incomparable wife Monty and me. God just opened a door, and we were nudged through it! *Small groups can be dynamite.* Power and growth in the Spirit thrive here. However, you must be particular. Many small groups simply do not address powerlessness, power, or honest, vulnerable sharing. Bible studies, as well, are wonderful, but can go on for years without an experience of real change. Groups can share other people's needs ad infinitum and can be powerful intercessory ministry, and yet no one ever shares personal struggles or vulnerabilities, which is a cover-up and hinders Holy Spirit Power.

Many small groups that you will encounter may have little or no *experience* with the Holy Spirit, or they may have simply failed to recognize Him knocking at their door. Sometimes the group chemistry is not conducive to these opportunities. I have found whole crowds of church people who apparently know as little about receiving the Holy Spirit as a non-churched person. All these groups have their purpose, and they do help people in their spiritual walks, but you are looking for something more. Keep looking. Keep asking God to lead you to the right people. Two is sometimes plenty. Jesus said where two or three are gathered in His Name, He would be there.[51]

Consider this. Suppose you wanted to learn to play tennis. You would find and associate yourself with someone who knows how to *play* tennis. Hanging with non-tennis players would not take you where you wanted to go, no matter how many films you watch, lectures you hear, discussions you have, or books you read. In finding your mentor, pray continuously for guidance. You will know! If you make a mistake, just gently move on. This is your life and, as you've heard, there is no dress rehearsal. **EXPLOSION:** the Master is at your service!

So why are so many churched people so uninvolved with the Holy Spirit? Perhaps they have not been taught, have not listened, or they *have declined to take the actions you and I are taking.* (The old willingness factor raises its bobbing head.) God adores these people—us—He does! He longs for them.

---

[51] Matt 18:20.

They appear to sit at the King's banquet table while suffering from spiritual anorexia. Guess what? God will be giving you and me a chance to share with some of these folk that there is more! He has a plan, and we have a part. However, we must pray that we are not exposed again to this spiritual anemia. I think it is contagious. I'm sure of it. If you "hang out" with them, (spiritually), you will wither!

On the other hand, be on the watch for that old serpent pride to come slithering out of the grass one day as we suddenly notice ourselves feeling "above" others rather than loving them, praying for them, and waiting for the right moment to share our struggles and discoveries with them. You may never want to make a speech, and you certainly will not have to hand out tracts on a corner. Your own journey told one on one, in your own words, will be the most powerful witness your listener might ever hear. **EXPLOSION:** if you are unwilling to share your excitement with another, you probably do not have much to share. **BACK TO BACK EXPLOSION:** As you share your journey with another, you will experience new revelations from God about yourself and your life! You will gain spiritual strength.

CHAPTER THIRTEEN

The Bible

I grew up in the church. I heard Scripture read every Sunday. I tried many times to read it, to make sense of it, but it just did not resonate with me. I felt as if I were reading gibberish. So I shelved it. My Bible gathered dust in my bookcase with the other just-to-look-at shelf fillers. Years went by. In the meantime, I married my college sweetheart, we had three glorious daughters, and now we have a Godly son-in-law and two of the finest young men on the planet for grandsons.

After shelving my Bible all those years ago, I still attended church every week. I was a church barnacle. I was just... attached. It was sometimes meaningful, but I did not really change. It never occurred to me that anything, particularly me, should be changing. Then, my infant third daughter became ill. We could not get a diagnosis, and all she could do was gasp for breath, whimper, and pull out her hair. Monty and I were beside ourselves. One afternoon, a lady driving our kids home in carpool inquired about our daughter and hearing there was no change, asked if she could pray for her. She left us some "tracts" on healing.

"Oh good grief!" That was my first thought when Monty told me about the conversation that evening. "Healing–get real! That was just for when Jesus was here." But something made me curious. I read the tracts. I was desperate. I took down that dusty Bible and tried to find the passages. That was not an easy assignment since I had no clue where the Book of James might be, or most of the others for that matter.

A short time later we were nudged into that group I mentioned earlier. We were astounded. These people believed that God still heals. To my befuddlement, they acted as if they had often discussed it with Him at length. They had experienced many problems and sorrows in their lives, but they possessed a joy, an assurance, a relationship with this mysterious God. They began to teach us. They prayed again for us to receive the Holy Spirit. We began to pray for our child, often several times a night. To our excitement and shock, gradually she began to improve. Usually when we prayed, upon our first, second, or third prayer time, she would become still. We looked at each other in wonder. Our group was not surprised in the least. They had been praying as well.

Eventually our prayers became as routine as cough syrup. We would keep praying until she calmed down, and we would trudge back to bed thanking God but no longer surprised. It was what He did. Let me say, however, our prayers did not always seem to work. We knew we were just conduits, and we knew sometimes the connection did not occur. We also knew that He had not abandoned us. We had the sense that He was

The Bible

---

still there, hoping we would continue to depend upon Him. We were hooked. We were not letting go, ever again.

I had noticed something right away, even being the spiritually challenged zombie that I was. These folks all had "study Bibles," new translations. They read them as if God Himself had written letters to them. All I had was my dusty old King James Bible. I went and bought a modern study Bible. When I opened it some days later, I was flabbergasted. The words leaped off the pages. They were speaking to my life…they were speaking to me. I thought "Whoa, what is this? Why have I never noticed this before?"

Dear ones: I believe the Holy Spirit was beginning to open the Scriptures to me. I could not stop reading. I gobbled the words. I did not need in- depth knowledge or at times even understanding. I just knew something had changed. Something powerful was happening to me. I did not *do anything* to bring about this change. I couldn't. Gradually, I understood that Someone was doing something!

Let me ask you a question: if you want to get close to someone, how can you do it without communicating – without knowing what they say, what they think, what they love? If you want to know God, does it not seem elementary to find out what He says, to receive His words daily? If you do not have one, get a modern translation study Bible – ask your mentor for a recommendation – and just start again. Ask the Holy Spirit to help you. He will. He is ecstatic you are beginning anew.

You do not have to start reading your new Bible from beginning to end. Start with John's gospel; then in no particular order read Acts, Romans, and the rest of the New Testament.

Read the Psalms. They are Holy Prayers. You will get to the Old Testament because it is important. Jesus is the fulfillment of everything in the Old Testament. You will want to learn the entire panorama of God's plan and history. And here is the best part: God will speak to you through these pages about everything – your problems, your relationships, your doubts and fears, your questions, and what He wants you to know and be. He will speak Truth to you, and you will lap up His words like a thirsty one finding a desert spring. I suspect God will speak personally to you more through your reading of Scripture than in any other manner! It is one more thing you will *know!* **EXPLOSION:** Read the words out loud, and feel what happens!

I do think your reading will be even more enlightening with a Bible commentary. There are many. Do not get bogged down in some thick tome that assumes you want to be a Bible scholar and need to know everything behind every sentence or what anybody ever thought or knew about the subject. Find a simple commentary for laymen. I have always loved the commentaries of William Barclay. They come in paperback, each book of the Bible is addressed separately, and they are written for the non-professional searcher. Also, there are fabulous Bible teachers today, in your town or nationally known. You can get DVD's or tapes, you can study in groups, or alone, even in the car. I have received untold amounts of Spiritual Drips of God into my veins while driving. The Holy Spirit will lead you. Ask around.

One more suggestion regarding Scripture: if your church pastor preaches more philosophy than sermons laced throughout with Scriptural foundations, I urge you to find an additional worship experience where you can hear the themes we are discussing expounded upon. *I am not saying leave your church.* Consider the possibility that God wants *you* to be a spiritual alchemist in that place. Ask God to lead you to an Oasis of Living Water. You will know when you experience a service with power. It moves you. It lifts you. It challenges and changes you. It will not be based upon the wisdom of man. It will not contradict or compromise Scripture. It will not be mush, and it certainly will not be boring.

CHAPTER FOURTEEN

Quiet Time

I am not sure how the Spirit will begin touching you. He may begin speaking to you through your Bible reading, or He may come to you in the Quiet. Quiet time and Bible reading are like a pair of gloves. Let us return to a similar question I asked you earlier: how does one become intimate with another? The answer is the same for a spiritual relationship as it is for a human relationship. You must spend time together.

Adored child of God, *Nothing, Nothing will spur your Steed of the Spirit like daily quiet time with God!* This is one of those **EXPLOSIONS:** a volcanic shift simply does not happen without the Holy Spirit Power taking hold of you. He does an intervention! Remember we talked about a new hunger for God? That is the Spirit moving! Now here is the stark truth: If you find you are not willing to commit to give God your time to be with Him *daily,* plead with Him to give you that willingness. **EXPLOSION:** The Holy Spirit *will not* push His way into your consciousness.

Quiet Time

You will make *personal contact* with Him only as you invite Him into your quiet room.

Now that you have become willing and have made a decision to set aside a quiet time with God every day, find a quiet place where you will be uninterrupted. You may have to set some boundaries with those around you about your privacy. Mornings seem easiest to manage for most folk, but there is no time rule here, except that your quiet time *must become a priority.* Start with a set time period; fifteen minutes is a start. You are not going to become still in a five- minute session.

"Bennett, I cannot just sit still for fifteen minutes. Maybe someday; but not yet." I know that. God knows that. The Spirit will be a wonderful trainer! As you begin, ask the Holy Spirit to come and teach you and empower you to receive. Now—that Bible and that simple commentary are wonderful starters. Add a simple daily meditation reading. There are hundreds of choices. I have some favorites: God Calling, Streams in the Desert, and My Utmost for His Highest.[52] Most Christian bookstores will have them in stock.

Dear one, this will be the oxygen of your new life! This daily quiet time will become your Living Water, and when you do not have it, you will find yourself feeling blue. I kid you not. This is when you will begin to make personal contact with the Great I Am – there is that promise again – this is when your doubts and confusion will accelerate their evaporation. This is when you will make the connection that will have you whispering

---

[52] God Calling Edited by A.J. Russell; Streams in the Desert, L.B. Cowman; My Utmost for His Highest, Oswald Chambers.

as Thomas did when he finally convinced himself Jesus was really raised from the dead, "My Lord and my God!"[53] Gradually, under the Power you will receive through your daily infilling, you will find yourself expanding this Time Together. It will not be a chore or an interruption of your day....it will be the Highlight of your day....not to have it will be like missing sleep.

We discussed earlier that our Holy Spirit Engagement can leak. Think of a car battery. It can gradually lose its power. It can go dead. **EXPLOSION:** *Your quiet time is your main recharging station! This is when God has re-entry access for your fill-up!*

---

[53] John 20:28 (NLT).

CHAPTER FIFTEEN

Writing Your Story

EXPLOSION: Another quiet time experience that will be yours and will be crucial help in your Homeward Journey is a written record. Go to an office supply store and purchase a bound blank-page notebook. I like non-columned accounting ledger books, anything that will hold up under some use and time. Legal pads and stenographer pads are just too temporary.

Regularly write down your struggles, your prayers, *answers to prayers,* and your thoughts about what you experienced in the day's quiet moments. This is not about whom you saw at lunch or who taught Sunday school. This is about what the Holy Spirit is doing in your life. It does not matter whether or not you consider yourself a "writer." What will happen as a result of these exercises is what matters. You will find there is something absolutely magical when thoughts and insights that you never knew were coming flow through your longhand.

Somehow the computer for me just is not the same. The act of hand to paper will seem to ignite your soul in some way.

Sometimes you will record your newest joy or understanding, sometimes the darkest depths of your despair. Be ruthlessly honest about what you write. No one is going to read it but you. You will challenge God, you will beg God, you will shake your fist at Him, and you will wear yourself out with Him. He is awaiting every question, every probe, and every plea! Keep listening. What did your daily readings say? Is He answering you? In your mind, what do you think He might be saying? Did you pick up one of your readings after you wrote in your journal and say, "Oh gosh, He is speaking to just what I wrote!"

I like to write His teachings, leadings, challenges, love talk, and answers in red ink. It helps me begin to see how natural our conversations are becoming. Sometimes He is absolutely quiet. I know if I wait, something will come, maybe in a few hours, a few days, a few years. I have created a record and I can wander back through the pages of His leading me, His presence with me, His carrying me, even when I thought I was totally alone and defeated.

Your journaling is a map that reminds you of the many twists and turns and highs and lows already traveled. Remember our talking about how we can leak Holy Spirit Power? You will uncover lessons and revelations in earlier journal entries that you have completely forgotten, and you will be re-strengthened as if they were new. **EXPLOSION:** Journaling becomes an experience of *writing to each other.* Can you believe something like this? Can you grasp what lies ahead of you through the Power of the Spirit? Do you begin to see how I could tell you when we started this, "You will *know."* Your journals will become a treasure. They are your story with God. Priceless.

A time will come when your quiet time will include just sitting with God. You will begin by letting the sediment in your mind begin to settle to the bottom, letting the water clear, and just "being" in His presence. I sometimes will say, "Is there anything You want to say, Lord?" And then I try to rest. Let the dervishes whirl wherever they are. They may not come in here. "Is there anyone I can serve for you today, Lord?" Sometimes something will come to mind, and I will jot it down and let it go. Sometimes He and I just relax together in quiet. Now, do not think I am any more anything than you. I am just like you. My will is reaching for Him regardless of the restlessness of my heart. I am visiting with Him. We were *created* for intimacy with Him. Intimacy with us is what He loves!

CHAPTER SIXTEEN

"Oh No!"

We have been talking about the changes we must make to stop resisting the Holy Spirit in transforming our lives. We have been talking about the things we somehow missed in our previous journey that numbed down our spiritual walks and made us almost "dead men walking." At least, at times that is what I felt. We have been stressing the critical importance of increasing our willingness as the one thing we already have the power to do. It is simply a matter of whether You Will, or *You Won't*.

It is time to talk now about another taboo subject…one most of us have not heard a lot about. I am talking about Confession. "Oh gads!" That was my response too. Do not skip this chapter. Do not resist the Holy Spirit! We are through with that. We are growing in obedience, we are growing in receptivity, and we are growing in our daily personal contact with God! It is time for your next Spirit Move!

Confession is a sacrament still observed in some churches, but most have all but abandoned it. I guess it is just not a very popular subject, so we, the church, have let it slide under the door to oblivion. Too bad. Too bad for us! You see, God originally inspired the writers of Scripture to command we confess to one another.[54] For hundreds of years, the church *knew* that Confession was required by God for our good: for our building up and for our healing.

Healing? How? Dear ones: Another sign that the Spirit is entering your life in a new and powerful way is that you will be convicted about yourself as never before. He is working! Ask Him if He desires your confession! Then watch for His answer. **EXPLOSION:** You will not make honest, thorough confession unless He is taking over, but now you are getting ready.

"So why, Bennett?" First, because God said to do it, and we are moving into obedience. That is enough if we want new Life. Would you believe I was sixty years old before I *was willing to receive* the revelation that it was my disobedience – my sin – that was causing me pain in my life? Hello? Secondly, our pride and fear have controlled us for far too long. We are coming to humility—surrender—and this is our path. Thirdly, if the only one who really knows all of your shadow side is God, you are still hiding. "Adam, where are you?" God called as He came walking in the Garden.[55] We have secrets, and our secrets are toxic to our spirits. They are walls that still stand between God

---

[54] James 5:16, 1st John 1:8-9.

[55] Gen 3:9.

and us. He will not push them down. He will not beg us. He asks us to tear them down; at least bring a hammer and chain.

Go get that list you hid when we started. It might need a little revision. Now write down, in code if you like, those things you decided not to reveal when you wrote them the first time. Pay very close attention to relationships with others and with yourself: resentments, anger, estrangement, dishonesty, selfishness, hurts, regrets, self-loathing, and shame. It is healing to speak the things that hurt you terribly, but do not allow yourself to wallow in blame or self- pity. You have played a part in the drama even if you have done nothing but hold on to the pain. Find it and own it. Be fiercely honest now. Leave out nothing. Have you discerned your idols? The Holy Spirit will shine His light on this darkness.[56] He is our Healer. We are done with hiding.

Good! Do you think the Holy Spirit was present by chance just then, or might you have resisted? Consider yourself one more time. Ask Him to step right into your hula hoop with you and help you not jump into someone else's. Have we not done that far too often? Jesus promised that His Holy Spirit would lead us into Truth.[57] He will. This is special time, Beloved! It is Holy Ground. Moses took off his shoes when he saw the Fire and heard a voice telling him he was standing on Holy Ground.[58]

---

[56] John 3:18-21, 8:12, 12:36, 46, 14:17.
[57] John 16:13.
[58] Ex 3:5, Josh 5:15

Now you are ready with the Power of the Spirit, to take a giant spiritual step. You would not have done this on a bet when we started this trip. Can you now feel the "draw?"

Somehow you know something important is happening to you. I want you to carefully seek out someone to hear your confession. Select someone you trust not to judge you and not to share your stuff with anyone. It may be your mentor. It might be a priest, minister, or therapist. It could be simply a very close friend. Do not choose someone who had involvement with you in these issues and might be hurt by some of the things you have to say.

Ask this person simply to hear you. He or she will not have to respond and will have no responsibility except to llisten in confidence. Constructive feed back would be a bonus! If this person has much life experience at all, you are not going to give him or her a shock. Despite how awful you think the things you must reveal are, the truth is you are pretty much like the rest of us. We are all just folks, and we pretty much get ourselves into similar quick-sand holes. Give yourself plenty of time when you meet. If one of you is in a hurry, you are going to walk away from the session still bearing that soul-tearing back-pack of secrets.

If you can be thoroughly honest, and leave nothing out, in time you will experience a new peace. It may be instantaneous, it may take a few days, but I believe you will experience a sense of *release!* **EXPLOSION:** You will have let go of your secrets, a huge step of surrender and you will have moved closer to God! It will be another example of knowing. You will know!

You may want to meet for another session at some point in the future. Having become aware of new baggage or some old stuff you had forgotten, be unrelentingly determined to amend your confession. Something keeps bubbling up, and you know it is the Spirit urging you to unpack! This time you will not carry the trepidation you felt before. The cleansing may even be something you eagerly anticipate. Pull down every wall! Enjoy the crash! "It is the Lord!"

CHAPTER SEVENTEEN

Restitution

I hear you wailing. I see your arms covering your head. I am reminded of trying to assist a wiggly worm off hot pavement back to the grass![59] Its tiny voice screams, "Leave me alone! Leave me alone!" Have we not acted out that cry to God for years? Try not to feel nauseated, and do not skip to the next topic, please. How do I know your reaction? Because I am the wiggliest of worms!!

Why must we address restitution? Well, if we are going to do our part of this life-changing, if we are going to obey what God has commanded, if we are serious about repentance, if we are going to continue to receive more and more of the Holy Spirit into ourselves, we do not have the luxury of side-stepping this action. Talk about walls! Pride comes crashing back upon us, like the spiritual equivalent to the Great Wall of China!

---

[59] I paraphrase a metaphor given by Pastor Chip Henderson, Pinelake Church, Flowood/Brandon, MS.

Restitution is a snake-stomper and old Mr. No Shoulders, whose game is Pride, will find an end to his coiled grip. We are becoming *willing* to do what we never would do before to assist God in creating our New Life.

Our Lord has something to say to us about restitution: "But I say if you are angry with someone, you are subject to judgment! ... So, if you are standing before the altar in the Temple offering a sacrifice to God and you suddenly remember that someone has something against you, leave your sacrifice there beside the altar. Go and be reconciled to that person. Then come and offer your sacrifice to God."[60] Sounds like He is saying, "You cannot be right with me while these issues hang out there." Gads! No wonder so many of us have remained spiritually anemic.

"OK, OK, how do I go about making restitution?" Ask for the Holy Spirit's power and guidance. As always, our own power is totally inadequate. We must engage in some more fierce introspection.

With whom are we in broken or damaged relationships? Make another list, this time of everyone who stirs negative emotions in your spirit. The most important ones—close friends, former friends, and family—are obvious. Put their names at the top of the list! Go back through your memory. Watch yourself for defensiveness and blame. That is the trap we have set for years with the inevitable result of ensnaring our own hearts. That has been our classic defocus maneuver. What part, no matter how small, did *you play* to keep the hurting alive? Did

---

[60] Matt 5:22a, 23-24 (NLT).

Restitution

you mistreat the person? Did you cheat or lie? Did you gossip? Did you rebel? Were you angry, defensive, irritable, ashamed, or abused? Were you simply selfish or wallowing in self-pity? Maybe you just turned and walked. That is one of my favorite ways to punish. Resentments are unfulfilled revenge!

What do you think this awareness in you might be doing to your life with the Holy Spirit? Uh-oh—I just received a holy nudge. I have been doing just what I have been describing to you. That is how I know how good we are at avoiding. We compartmentalize like crazy. Unfortunately, the one who is made crazy is you-know-who. We have constructed our own wall between God and ourselves, and we are consuming the poison and assuming the other person will die.

Without allowing you to slip this noose, good judgment is necessary. There are times when to bring up an old wound will bring new harm to the other person or people closely connected. Do not inflict more pain in your attempt to resolve old pain. Some of these people may be dead or unreachable. Consider writing them a letter even though they cannot receive it. Whenever possible, and notice I did not use the term "convenient," you will want to meet person to person. If you really cannot, a letter will have to suffice.

The way I suggest you handle the situation is to call the person and ask if you might come by for a few minutes. The answer usually will be either yes, or why. If the answer is no, then your business is finished for the time being. Just say thank you and make your exit. Things may change as the Spirit does His work. If you have to answer the "why," say what you plan to say in person. When you do have the opportunity to meet, simply explain that you have felt some pain about the way things have gone and you would like to talk. Then, without any reference to what the person did or did not do, explain that you feel you had a role in what happened—you don't have to relive the incident unless the person doesn't remember or has no knowledge of what happened.

Explain that you would like to express your regret and see if there is anything you can do to make things right. Then hush. You do not need to go on and on. Listen to what the person has to say, even if you are being berated. Go back to your simple question if things run off on a side road. Holding your emotions in check as best you can, ask, "Is there anything I can do to make this right?" If a suggestion or demand is made either decide your answer, or if you need to, ask if you can consider the request and come back. Follow up. Do not just forget to return. Often times, you will be surprised by a softer response than you expected. You do not have to stick around once you have had your say. Offer your thanks and leave. Remember, the response is the other person's business, not yours. You are responsible only for you! You dressed out and showed up. Let the Holy Spirit take responsibility for the outcome.[61]

Obviously, restitution will take time if your list is long. Address the important conflicts first, not later. In a few cases, the timing may have to wait. Ask the Holy Spirit to make a way. The point is you are tearing down the walls that have hindered your intimacy with God for too long. More new Creation is on the way!

---

[61] Rev. Edwin Bacon at The Cathedral of St. Andrew, Jackson, MS.

CHAPTER EIGHTEEN

Prayer

A few months into your new journey and under your daily requesting and receiving His Power; you are going to notice a change in your prayer life. Suggestions about prayer are not going to be necessary. The reason is that by then, you will be discussing just about every detail of your life with your most trusted Guide and Teacher. God will become your number one Confidant. You will be talking frequently with your Abba, the Biblical name that may be translated, "Papa."[62]

EXPLOSION: Intimacy is now something you experience. It is another new thing you *know!* The Scripture includes many prayers and much instruction. You will be led to them and drink them with gusto. You are, I hope, continuing to start and end your days on your knees. Stay in that mode. I do offer some age-old suggestions: morning prayers should include asking for His guidance in your thoughts and actions this day and

---
[62] Rom 8:15.

reminding Him that you are searching *only* for His will in all things. Ask Him to send His Holy Spirit to empower you. He has not forgotten that you cannot do anything without Him.

Ask Him to give you the power to abide only in Him for all your needs[63] and to show you how you can serve others for Him today. Ask the Holy Spirit to open your eyes, ears, and heart to His voice. By all means, add specific intercessions and requests, expect them to be forthcoming, and offer Him your thanks, love, and adoration. In the event of down periods, write a gratitude list – the most powerful ones are the intangibles. Keep this list daily and mention it in your prayers. **EXPLOSION:** More Power resides in gratitude. I would not make this up! It is ALL in the Scriptures which are actually our Letters from Home.[64]

Throughout the day, continue this ongoing conversation. Do not do all the talking. If you ask Him a specific question, He WILL answer, if not immediately, eventually. Do not forget, "no" is an answer. When He says no, you can trust that He has something in mind. Often what we sense as "no" may really be "not yet." However, learning to accept His "no" with confidence is spirit power personified, but you *must* be a listener.

We are learning to tune our receivers to eliminate the static. Concentrate on being obedient to what you feel He is telling you. I do not mean audible voices. Ponder what you hear in Scripture and with your mentor and in your quiet time, your journaling, your Holy Imagination. Imagination is God's gift,

---

[63] John 15:1-8.

[64] Proverbs 17:22, 15:15.

our spiritual transmitter. You are experiencing new blockbuster change and more Living Water. Can you not feel your life moving at last? In your evening prayers, look back over your day with Him. Be honest about the good and the not so good. Were you able to serve someone? Were you able to speak to someone about the One you know, about the Power? Did that person need encouragement, help, prayer, or just someone to listen?

The gospel is, I believe, boiled down to its essence in John 15 in three words: "Abide in Me." Did you feel as if you were able to "abide?" Read that chapter repeatedly. Your reading will become another form of prayer! Were you praying today for His will instead of yours? Were you resentful, scared, sad, angry, hurtful, dishonest, envious, lustful, or selfish? What alterations of heart are needed? Do you need to make repairs to a relationship? Review your victories as well! You did Spirit empowered things today. When power was needed, you knew who had the power, and it was not you! Whew! What a relief!! Remember, Dear one, these disciplines are explosive, but not if you slip back to your old life! You are on the move—a Holy Spirit Transformation is in process! Persist. The miracles are beginning. Your new prayer life is explosive. Be disciplined about these disciplines!! Keep depending on His assistance.

Remember this **(EXPLOSION): w**hen you pray expectantly in accordance with His will, unselfishly, and your heart abides under the "shadow of the Almighty,"[65] orders are issued in Heaven.[66] Acknowledge them, rest in them, stand firm on them.

I occasionally hear myself thinking about what appears to be unanswered prayers. I also find myself taking lightly the multitude of my requests that He *answers in boldness*. What's with that? He says "yes" continuously, and we are oblivious. We seem riveted to what we believe to be "no." Look back. Issues have been resolved by the train-load. Your journal will not lie. He carries us when we think we are walking the plank. He is holding us when we are fighting to free ourselves from some hopeless web. Know that the Spirit is waking us up to answered prayer. He has been leading you to this! The Banquet Table just keeps growing more extravagant!

Paul said in his encouragement to the Ephesians: "Don't worry about anything; instead pray about everything. Tell God what you need, and thank Him for all He has done. If you do this, you will experience God's peace, which is far more wonderful than the human mind can understand. His peace will guard your hearts and minds as you live in Christ Jesus. And this same God who takes care of me will supply all your needs from His glorious riches, which have been given to us in Christ Jesus. Now glory be to God our Father forever and ever."[67]

Consider another of Paul's wonderful prayers for you this minute, this hour, today. Let it flood your heart and soul:

---

[65] Psa 91:1.

[66] Dan 9:23, 10-12, John 14:12-14.

[67] Eph 4:6-7, 19 (NLT).

Ever since I first heard of your strong faith in the Lord Jesus, and your love for Christians everywhere, I have never stopped thanking God for you. I pray for you constantly, asking God, the glorious Father of our Lord Jesus Christ, to give you spiritual wisdom and understanding, so that you might grow in your knowledge of God. I pray that your heart will be flooded with light so that you can understand the wonderful future He Has promised to those He called. I want you to realize what a rich and glorious inheritance He has given to you. I pray that you will begin to understand the incredible greatness of His power for us who believe Him. This is the same mighty power that raised Christ from the dead and seated Him in the place of honor at God's right hand in the heavenly realms. Now He is far above any ruler or authority or power or leader or anything else in this world or in the world to come. And God has put all things under the authority of Christ, and He gave Him this authority for the benefit of the church. And the church is His body; it is filled by Christ, who fills everything everywhere with His presence."[68]

---

[68] Eph 1:15-23 (NLT).

Do you see it? Embrace it! Paul wants you to understand about the Power! It is your inheritance! It is yours for the receiving! It is a Power that fills you with His presence! It changes *everything!* You will NEVER be the same!

Stop now. Be still and feel His Presence. He is in you. He is pouring His Presence into you, more and more. Be at peace. Do you sense it? You are partaking of the joy of what it means to be a child of God!

CHAPTER NINETEEN
Gratitude

I mentioned this earlier, but gratitude deserves a chapter of its own. Nothing is better for keeping you alert to God's tender presence than the habit of gratitude. He places signs for those who have eyes to see, and they are ready and waiting for you day and night. We get so busy with routine, anxiety, and self, we pass by thousands of greetings posted by God each day. The sun rises in glory while the birds sing their praises, or the clouds roll in majesty and pour life giving moisture to all of waiting life. You smell coffee and bacon, you read a Psalm, and you wiggle into your favorite old sweater.

Look around. Children are wide eyed, squealing, and full of giggles. Moms and grandpas are caressing their loved ones. Wagging tailed dogs and aloof stretching cats and wondrous spider webs await your enjoyment. Kneel down in the grass and discover the tiny universe God has placed there in perfection and beauty. A fish suddenly breaks the surface and soars as if to fly. Friends are waiting to talk, to love and comfort each other. Oh, music! Music is processed through our hearts rather than our intellect. Listen and be lifted. Dance and sing loud. God is near you and now you know.

Make your own list of one hundred grateful favorites. Post it where you will see it every day and allow it to assist you in resisting the spiritual amnesia that plagues us, beckoning us into a false abyss. **EXPLOSION:** That feeling of darkness is The Liar. His initial goal is to convince you he is not there. He wants your spiritual death, to tell you that you are alone and without Help.[69] Spit in his face, speak the name of Jesus, and call for your army of Heavenly Hosts.[70] They are yours to command because you are an heir to the Throne.

When depression and drudgery invade, ask The Holy Spirit for gratitude. Sit in silence and hear God's words of encouragement, love, and power. Use your Holy Imagination to hear Him speaking. Give thanks that He is teaching you to make personal contact with Him. **EXPLOSION:** The only one who is glad for your guilt, shame, and hopelessness is the Duke of Darkness. You sometimes don't have a choice about your feelings, but you can choose your actions. Decide to get positive. Act as if. Act as if He is carrying you in his arms until you can soar like an eagle.[71] I don't know the source, but I keep the following Blessing from God near at hand because I forget what He wants me to remember:

---

[69] John 8:43-44 10:10.

[70] Luke 2:13.

[71] Isa 40:11, 29-31, Rom 15:13.

Gratitude

You may not know me, but I know everything about you (Psa 139:1).

I know when you sit down and when you rise up (Psa 139:2).

I am familiar with all your ways (Psa 139:3).

Even the very hairs on your head are numbered (Matt 10:29-30).

For you were made in My image (Gen 1:27).

In Me you live and move and have your being. For you are my offspring (Acts 17:28).

I knew you before you were conceived (Jer 1:4-5).

I chose you when I planned creation (Eph 1:11-12).

You were no mistake, for all your days are written in My book (Psa 139:15-16).

I determined the exact time of your birth and where you would live (Acts 17:26).

You are fearfully and wonderfully made (Psa 139:14).

I knit you together in your mother's womb (Psa 139:13).

And brought you forth on the day you were born (Psa 71:6).

I have been misrepresented by those who don't know Me (John 8:41-44).

I am not distant and angry, but am the complete expression of love (1st John 4:16).

And it is My desire to lavish My love on you (1st John 3:1)

Simply because you are My child and I am your Father (1st John 3:7).

I offer you more than your earthly father ever could (Matt 7:11).

For I am the perfect Father (Matt 5:48).

Every good gift you receive comes from My hand (James 1:17).

For I am your Provider and I meet your needs (Matt 6:31-33).

My plan for your future has always been filled with hope (Jer 29:11).
Because I love you with an everlasting love (Jer 31:3).
My thoughts toward you are countless as the sand on the seashore (Psa 139:17-18).
And I rejoice over you with singing (Zep 3:17).
I will never stop doing good to you (Jer 32:40).
For you are my treasured possession (Ex 19:5).
I desire to establish you with all my heart and all my soul (Jer 32:41).
And I want to show you great and marvelous things. (Jer 33:3)
For if you seek Me with all your heart, you will find Me (Deut 4:29).
So, delight in Me and I will give you the desires of your heart (Psa 37:4).
For it is I who gave you those desires (Phil 2:13).
I am able to do more for you than you could possibly imagine (Eph 3:20).
For I am your greatest encourager (2nd Thes 2:16-17).
I am also the Father who comforts you in all your troubles (2nd Cor 1:3-4).
When you are brokenhearted, I am close to you (Psa 34:18).
As a shepherd carries a lamb, I have carried you close to My heart (Isa 40:11).
One day I will wipe away every tear from your eyes. And I will take away all the pain you have suffered on this earth (Rev 21:3-4).
I am your Father, and I love you even as I love my son, Jesus (John 17:23).

For in Jesus, my love for you is revealed (John 17:26).
And to tell you that I am not counting your sins, Jesus died so that you and I could be reconciled (2nd Cor 5:18-19).
His death was the ultimate expression of my love for you (1st John 4:10).
I gave up everything I loved that I might gain your love (Rom 8:31-32).
If you receive the gift of my son Jesus, you receive Me (1st John 2:23).
And nothing will ever separate you from my love again (Rom 8:38-39).
When it's time for you to come Home, I'll throw the biggest party heaven has ever seen (Luke 15:7).
I have always been your Father, and I will always be your Father (Eph 3:14-15).
My question is…Will you be my child? (John 1:12-13).
I am waiting for you (Luke 15:11-32).
With Love, Your Father, Almighty God

If I still cannot touch gratitude after reading this letter from my Papa, I check my pulse.

CHAPTER TWENTY

More and More

Continue to do your repentance and participate with Him as you struggle/emerge from worm to butterfly. This process is not instantaneous. Look around. Life grows. Pray daily for more of Him. There will be setbacks. There will continue to be pain. The wine cannot be made without the crushing of the grapes. Our surrender is His desire. So why is surrender so hard? You know the answer: we do not want to surrender. Not all the way. We have divided hearts. We are resistant to being "all in."

Pray with persistence and expectation *every day* for His Power to help you surrender your will to His. Jesus gave you His oath that "When you seek Me, *with all your heart,* you will find Me." "Ask," He says, "and it will be given." Pray for His Power that you may come to acceptance of your life and all of its twists and turns. **EXPLOSION:** Whenever you are anxious or irritable, look for your unacceptance. We said it earlier: the pain is in the resistance! He is continually molding us. He loves the image of clay in the hands of the Potter.[72] When Jesus was facing the undeserved torture and death that lay ahead, His thought was, "Shall I not drink from the cup the Father has given Me?"[73] I ponder that thought often as I wage my continuous war to accept.

Listen once again to Paul's plea: "So I advise you to live according to your new life in the Holy Spirit. Then you won't be doing what your sinful nature craves. The old sinful nature loves to do evil, which is just the opposite of what the Holy Spirit wants. And the Spirit gives us desires that are opposite from what the sinful nature desires. These two forces are constantly fighting each other, and our choices are never entirely free from this conflict."[74]

One of my mentors used to remind us that after victory was declared in Europe during World War II, there were still "clean up" battles springing up here and there. Our experience is the same. The war is won….Christ is in you and that is your assurance of Glory![75] Mop-up skirmishes will continue. Do not be shocked. You might enjoy a pink cloud of Spirit Presence, and then, to your dismay, He may seem to withdraw. He has not. He desires to strengthen your faith. He intends to make you strong! Consider the constant attacks and the final torture God required of His own son! When He knows you are His, He

---

[72] Jer 18: 1-6.
[73] John 18:11 (NLT).
[74] Gal 5:16-17.
[75] Col 1:27.

often asks you to endure trials. If your heart is broken, *act as if* He has not left. *Act as if* your heart has not faltered!

EXPLOSION: As you act as if, lean on your faith community and cling to God. Even though your heart may feel crushed, your faith will not only return, but you will develop the wonderful faith muscles He intends during these times of trial or emptiness. These gifts we are receiving even *through storms* enhance the process of our wonderful transformation. They will gradually bring us to fall on our knees in joy and thanksgiving; knowing we never have to go back to our old, dry, frail life.

CHAPTER TWENTY ONE

Every Day is Christmas

Here is a final exclamation point on the Surprise I promised was waiting around the corner. The Spirit that lives in us has unimaginable gifts, ones we might have thought impossible to receive. They are not for sale. They are available only through this new Power that now moves within you. In the fifth chapter of Galatians Paul writes, "when the Holy Spirit controls our lives, He will produce in us the fruits of the Spirit: love, joy, peace, patience, kindness, goodness, faithfulness, gentleness, and self-control."[76]

Did you notice the first three fruits? Gifts! Priceless, Free, Grace! This Third Person of the Trinity, the Holy Spirit, is out of the shadows forever now, and we will never let go again. Love! God *is* Love. What is that about? It is not just that His love for us is unfathomable. As your newly discovered love for Him, others, and yourself *gradually* grows *through* the power

---

[76] Gal 5:22 (NLT).

of the Spirit, you will notice something else. **EXPLOSION:** It is this power based Spirit-love that acts as a millstone, gradually grinding to powder that former self-absorbed love.

Have you noticed how often I use the word "gradual"?[77] Adored one, however slowly, *now* your spirit sees no turning back! You may not see it in yourself because self is shriveling, but others will. However, Peace and Joy will quietly slip in with the other Galatians-described gifts attached as we become branches in Him who is the Vine. A new Life of serenity is embracing you. No more words! *Experience* is enveloping us in new and mysterious ways!.[78]

Listen again to Paul: "Since we believe that Christ died for everyone, we also believe that *we have all died to the old life we used to live.* He died for everyone *so that those who receive his new life will no longer live to please themselves. Instead they will live to please Christ, who died and was raised for them.*"[79]

These gifts are coming to you, sometimes surprisingly quickly, sometimes gradually, but you will never again wonder if your faith is mist or myth. Notice the first fruit: love. All the ones that follow in that Galatians list are the manifestations of the first. Love is the Prize: love for our Lord, healthy love for ourselves, and love for our neighbors. Find your way to 1 Corinthians 13. You may have read or heard these verses many times, or you may not have. As the Holy Spirit takes

---

[77] Hab 2:3.

[78] Eph 3:20.

[79] 2nd Cor 5:14-15 (NLT).

His residence in you, these words no longer seem of another world. They become our ideal, not something still beyond you, but something we can honestly and objectively embrace. It is your heart! It is Holy Spirit Power.

CHAPTER TWENTY TWO

You Are A New Creation!

Child of the Alpha and the Omega, when we began this time together, I told you that we were going to leave the misty flats of anemic faith behind. I told you that the surprise that was coming to you would be definitive and experiential. No more talk. I promised "walk." Action. Change. New life. Power. Paul promised the same experience more than 2,000 years ago: "What counts is whether we really have been changed into new and different people."[80] "For the Kingdom of God is not just fancy talk; it is *living by God's power!*"[81]

We began by wondering why we had missed the "new creation" that people of God were supposed to experience. I confessed being a Christian without any measurable transformation for many years! I admitted I needed more power than I possessed if I were to seek and find God. We all asked, "And

---

[80] Gal 6:15 (NLT).

[81] 1st Cor 4:20 (NLT).

what am I to do about that?" That has been our conundrum, has it not? Jesus told Nicodemus something miraculous had to happen as a *prerequisite* to entering the Kingdom.[82] Just like old Nick, we said, "How? I can't! What am I to do?" *Now you know the answer to that question.* The Holy Spirit is doing for you what you never dreamed. It takes time, but you *know already* something is happening! You ARE BECOMING a new creation! Receive it![83] You will not let go. You will ask for more and more, you can never be full enough!

Jesus prayed for us when He was praying for His disciples near the end of His time with them. Feast on His words as He speaks to His Father:

> I have told these men about you. They were in the world, *but then You gave them to Me. Actually, they were always Yours, and You gave them to Me;* and they have kept your Word. Now they know that everything I have is a gift from You, for I have passed on to them the words You gave me; *and they accepted them and know that I came from You, and they believe You sent me.* My prayer is not for the world, but for those you have given me, because *they belong to You; and You have given them back to Me, so they are My glory!*

---

[82] John 3:3-8.

[83] 2nd Cor 5:17.

Now I am departing the world; I am leaving them behind and coming to You. Holy Father, keep them and care for them—all those You have given Me – so that they will be united just as We are. During My time here, I have kept them safe. I guarded them so that not one was lost, except the one headed for destruction, as the Scriptures foretold. And now I am coming to You. I have told them many things while I was with them *so they would be filled with My joy.* I have given them Your word. And the world hates them because they do not belong to the world, just as I do not. I'm not asking you to take them out of the world, but to keep them safe from the evil one. They are not part of this world any more than I am. *Make them pure and holy by teaching them Your words of truth.*

As You sent Me into the world, I am sending them into the world. *And I give Myself entirely to You so they also might be entirely Yours. I am praying not only for these disciples* **but for all who will ever believe in Me because of their testimony. My prayer for all of them is that they will be one, just as You and I are one, Father – that just as you are in me and I am in You, so they will believe in Us and the world will believe that You sent Me. I have given them the glory You gave Me, so that they may be one as We are – I in them and You in Me,**

> **all being perfected into one.** Then the world will know that You sent Me and will understand that *You love them as much as You love Me.* Father, I want these whom You have given Me *to be with Me, so they can see My glory!* You gave Me the glory because You loved Me even before the world began! O righteous Father, *the world doesn't know You, but I do; and these disciples know You sent Me.* **And I have revealed You to them and will keep on revealing You. I will do this so that Your love for Me may be in them and I in them.** (John 17, NLT).

God the Son is praying to God the Father, that through The Holy Spirit, we may become grafted to Him, becoming One with Him, drawing ever closer to the Kingdom of God.

So what about these "fruits of the Spirit" in the fifth chapter of Galatians that to many of us sound so pious, so much beyond our reach and experience? Peace: my understanding develops and changes, but today I would describe it as having little to do with smooth waters. We *must* experience the storms … the shipbuilder did not create his vessel to rest safely in the harbor. Only the raging waters can strengthen our faith. The peace that passes understanding comes to me from the unshakable *experience* that He is in my little boat with me, always, whispering His promises of faithfulness and victory during the storms as the waves bludgeon me and attempt to suck me under. Oh yes I still panic. My spiritual amnesia **storms** the boat, and I wail and tremble. That does not change the fact that He is right here with me, and I am learning to quiet myself and hear His tender assurance.

And Joy, what about Joy? Well, it is not giddiness. For me, it is My Lover's embrace, my arms around Him, His around me—an ecstasy words cannot describe. He will continue to whisper, "My Child, you didn't choose Me, I chose You. You are my masterpiece. You are Mine! I will never fail you. I will never forsake you!"[84]

The others...patience, kindness, goodness, faithfulness, gentleness, and self-control, you will find, as I have, that they are somewhere inside you. At times, pain will be the soil in which they mature. Hard times are an unavoidable part of life. When they come, cling to Him all the more. Yield to Him. Draw closer than ever. **EXPLOSION:** Some of the most powerful and exquisite moments of making personal contact with your Lord and Savior will come during your darkest hours. His whisper of reassurance, of His continued care, His overcoming all will lift you, and you will wonder how people who have not discovered what you have discovered can possibly go on.

In retrospect, you will know you are changing; you may not feel the growth at the time it is happening, just as you were unaware of your physical growth. As the days and years pass, and as you continue to want all of Him you can receive, as you continue praying daily to be filled with His Spirit, He will do what He has promised.[85] His will and your will are now being

---

[84] John 15:16, Isa 43:1, Heb 13:5.
[85] John 14: 15-18

grafted as Vine and Branch. A graft almost always requires a wound—pain. We talked about that.

Understand this: there is an Opposing Force that wants to convince you that you are not worthy, are not growing, are not receiving Power. He has disciples who insist your faith is self-delusion. But he is already "whupped," as we say down South. The metaphor comparing the Spirit gifts to fruit implies that others will partake and benefit from your gifts. You will know you have been touched by God—changed, redeemed—and others will know as He allows His Living Water to flow through you.

"Bennett, I know now that I am receiving; I know that I am growing; I sense that I am being changed… it is gradual and I understand that slow growth principle. Tell me the rest! Are there more signs of my Spirit Intervention? Are there more ways to *KNOW?*" Yippee and Honor and Glory! I'm so thrilled for your hunger. If you are relentlessly doing the repentance/change disciplines we have discussed, you *cannot keep from being transformed,* and you *will feel this transformation!* This has been God's plan for you all along.[86]

EXPLOSION: One more powerful and obvious manifestation of your New Creation is that your "want to" factor is becoming a "got to" factor! You will find yourself having moved from wanting more of God to "I have GOT to have ALL of Him!" Psalm 42:1 describes our souls as being like a deer panting for water! Dear one, observe your heart; you will have no doubt.

---

[86] Rom 8:29-30, Eph 1:9, 13-14, Col 1:19-23, Titus 2:11-15, 1st Peter 1:2, 2:9-10, 2nd Peter 1:3, 1st John 2:27, Rev 1:8.

EXPLOSION: God has given you another mysterious, miraculous, gift: "He is working in you, giving you the *desire* to obey Him and the **Power** to do what pleases Him!"[87] **He is doing the work. You have become willing. You have become hungry. You have stopped doing nothing. Repentance, confession, obedience, surrender, and intimacy have become your will. You are all in. You will not retreat. Now, the walls are collapsing that have barred you from His power. He is moving in and is doing His holy intervention in you. It is His work to do. It is what He has always dreamed for you.**

Now you know what you know, and as the months and years unfold to you these precious Kingdom secrets, you will arrive at your own God-given wisdom. To paraphrase Oswald Chambers, as we search for the Holy Destination for our lives, what we imagined as the "end" is not what God has in mind. What we call the journey, the process, the intimate Relationship, *that* God calls the end. You are falling into the most exotic, enduring, rewarding, exhilarating, and lifesaving love affair of your Life! Hang on no matter what! Remember this Truth: He is either everything, or He is nothing.[88] This faith of ours, your knowing, is your gift from God. "For the Kingdom of God is not just fancy talk; it is living by God's power. Which do you choose?"[89] "Indeed, God is ready to help you right now. **Today** is the day of salvation."[90] HALLALUJAH!

---

[87] Phil 2:13 (NLT).

[88] This stark truth is quoted from the "Big Book" of Alcoholics Anonymous.

[89] 1st Cor 4: 20-21 (NLT).

[90] 2nd Cor 6:2 (NLT).

"I came to you in weakness—timid and trembling.
And my message and my preaching were very plain.
I did not use wise and persuasive speeches,
but the Holy Spirit was powerful among you.
I did this so you might trust the power of God
rather than human wisdom."
1st Cor 2:3-5 (NLT)

"When I think of the wisdom and scope of God's plan,
I fall to my knees and pray to the Father,
The Creator of everything in heaven and on earth.
I pray that from His glorious, unlimited resources
He will give you mighty inner strength through His Holy Spirit.
And I pray that Christ will be more and more at home in
your hearts
as you trust in Him.
May your roots go down deep into the soil of God's marvelous love.
And may you have the power to understand,
as all God's people should, how wide, how long, how high
and how deep
His love really is.
May you experience the love of Christ, though it is so great
you will never fully understand it.
Then you will be filled with the fullness of life and power
that comes from God."
Ephesians 3:14-19 (NLT)

www.ingramcontent.com/pod-product-compliance
Ingram Content Group UK Ltd.
Pitfield, Milton Keynes, MK11 3LW, UK
UKHW041954230426
12048UKWH00008B/324